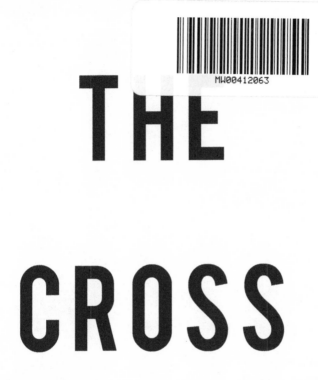

THE

CROSS

DR. KRIS SEGREST

Cover Design: Kristin Odom
Interior Design: Cody Knight

Printed by CreateSpace, An Amazon.com Company
Available on Kindle and other devices

All Scripture is from the English Standard Version (ESV) unless
otherwise noted.
All emphasis has been added by the author.

ACKNOWLEDGMENT

To the staff team of First Baptist Church of Wylie, TX
It is a joy to call each of you a friend and co-laborer in
the Gospel.
May the Lord keep His hand of favor upon each of you.

CONTENTS

FOREWORD

*I**F THE AVERAGE** person, in the time of Jesus Christ, walked around in our day, they would be blown away by many things. Obviously, electronics of every sort would be fascinating. Machines that fly people all over the world in a matter of hours would be a wonder. Entertainment venues that make the Coliseum in Rome feel small would impress. Yet, the one thing that would absolutely dumbfound the ancients is why so many people wear, display, even tattoo their ancient device of death and torture on their bodies and homes. I am talking about the cross.

The cross was the equivalent to the modern-day

electric chair. No one could fathom having jewelry, décor in a house, a t-shirt or a tattoo of an electric chair. Why would people today use a cross as decoration?

You must remember that 2,000 years has passed since Jesus hung on a cross one Friday. In our modern times, the pain, heartache, stigma, abuse and death the cross rendered is passé. Today, the cruelest instrument of death throughout all time is simply a decoration. Whether it be a ceramic cross for a home display, a gold necklace lined with precious jewels, or decal on an automobile, we have lost the real significance of the cross.

Standing over ten feet high and weighing over 300 pounds, the cross was an imposing instrument of death. This method of execution was reserved for the worst of the worst. Crucifixions were held in the most public of places to incite fear into would-be law breakers. The vertical beam was normally a fixture at the sight of the executions. The horizontal beam, or patibulum, weighed 125 pounds and was carried by the criminal from the place of sentencing to the sight of the execution. The process of death by crucifixion lasted for hours up to days. It literally sucked the life out by suffocating the condemned.

Jesus died for the sins of the world so that men and God might have a relationship together. Of all the ways Jesus could have died, He died on the vilest of execution apparatuses. Demonstrating the ugliness of sin and God's judgment against it. In this work, we will rediscover why the cross matters. This ancient instrument of death has much to teach us about our relationship to Christ, His Father and the freedom we received.

For even the Son of Man came not to be served but to serve, and to give his life as a ransom for many.

Mark 10:45

"By Christ's purchasing redemption, two things are intended: his satisfaction and his merit; the one pays our debt, and so satisfies; the other procures our title, and so merits. The satisfaction of Christ is to free us from misery; the merit of Christ is to purchase happiness for us."

Jonathan Edwards

OUR RANSOM
PROVIDED

*I*N *1973, THE* richest man in the world was American Oil tycoon, J. Paul Getty. He was worth 1.9 billion dollars. In that same year, his grandson, John Paul Getty III, was kidnapped, when he was 16-years-old. His kidnappers wanted a ransom of 17 million dollars. J. Paul Getty refused to pay the ransom for his grandson, resulting in the kidnappers cutting off the boy's right ear. By the age of 24, his grandson, due to the ordeal he suffered, the neglect he experienced in later years, and a growing drug habit, ended up becoming paralyzed. J. Paul Getty's money was of no use because he was a notorious tightwad. At his palatial mansion in England, he had a pay phone that he forced his guests and family to use, this is the definition of a tightwad.

When you consider the extravagant price that Jesus paid to ransom you, it is priceless. He was not stingy in anyway, he was lavish in his price. To be clear, Jesus did not pay off Satan for you. Instead, Jesus destroyed Satan's power over death "…that through death he might destroy the one who has the power of death, that is, the devil." (Hebrews 2:14) Satan has no claim to you anymore.

So, who did Jesus pay off? It was no one other than God Himself. Ephesians 5:2 says, "And walk in love, as Christ loved us and gave himself up for us, a fragrant offering and sacrifice to God." Jesus paid off the ransom price of sin to satisfy the demand of God, His Father. What we are saved from is the judgment of God.

Who are the 'many' the verse above refers to? Obviously, the blood of Jesus was enough for the ransom of everyone who has ever lived on planet earth. Yet, not everyone will accept Christ as their Savior and Lord. Therefore, Christ's sacrifice is potentially enough for all, but not operative for all. 1 Timothy 2:5-6 says, "For there is one God, and there is one mediator between God and men, the man Christ Jesus, who gave himself as a ransom for all, which is the testimony given at the proper time." The ransom for you was provided on the cross, will you walk in it?

<u>Reflections</u>

Have you been ransomed from the captivity of sin through Christ's sacrifice? If so, what was it?

How does it feel to know God paid the price for you, even though the price was His only Son?

Who do you know needs to be freed from sin? How can you be used to help them accept Christ?

For everyone has sinned; we all fall short of God's glorious standard. Yet God, in his grace, freely makes us right in his sight. He did this through Christ Jesus when he freed us from the penalty for our sins. For God presented Jesus as the sacrifice for sin. People are made right with God when they believe that Jesus sacrificed his life, shedding his blood. This sacrifice shows that God was being fair when he held back and did not punish those who sinned in times past, for he was looking ahead and including them in what he would do in this present time. God did this to demonstrate his righteousness, for he himself is fair and just, and he makes sinners right in his sight when they believe in Jesus.

Romans 3:23-26 (NLT)

"It was not nails that held Jesus to that wretched cross; it was his unqualified resolution, out of love for his Father, to do his Father's will—and it was his love for sinners like me"

D.A. Carson

JESUS TAKES OUR PUNISHMENT

ONE TIME, WHEN my son was young, he was acting up. The behavior continued to the point that he needed a spanking. He obviously was not thrilled about this punishment and he began to cry, even before the spanking. So, in a moment of what seemed to be parenting genius, I told him I would take his punishment for him. I thought that he would see the valiant sacrifice I was making on his behalf. I gave him the plastic spatula, which was our method of punishment, and told him to spank me in his place. Well, with all the zeal and power that a little kid can muster, he went to town on me. The point of my lesson, completely lost.

You realize that you have sinned… Right? You understand that nothing you can do will make up for the reality that your sins separate you from God and that you deserve eternal separation from God in a place called Hell. While we might compromise our standards, God never compromises His. God will never allow sin into His perfect presence.

There is a part of us that does not like to think that a loving God could be so harsh. Most people like the gracious and loving part of God and do not like or want to accept His wrath and judgment toward sin. Yet, his love and his wrath are like two sides of the same coin. Both are necessary. God's love means little and Christ's sacrifice means nothing if there is no consequence for our sins. If everyone goes to Heaven, then why was it even necessary for Christ to die? Yet, sin is real. Heaven and Hell are certain. Either you die for your sins or Christ dies for your sins. Isn't Jesus wonderful for taking our punishment? Let us respond correctly.

<u>Reflections</u>

Did you ever get 'set free' for something you deserved to be punished for?

Have you ever taken anyone else's punishment?

How should knowing Jesus took your punishment change your attitude toward people?

For if while we were enemies we were reconciled to God by the death of his Son, much more, now that we are reconciled, shall we be saved by his life. More than that, we also rejoice in God through our Lord Jesus Christ, through whom we have now received reconciliation.

Romans 5:10-11

The very God whom we have offended has Himself provided the way whereby the offence has been dealt with. His anger, His wrath against the sin and the sinner, has been satisfied, appeased and he therefore can now reconcile man unto Himself.

Martin Lloyd-Jones

RECONCILES US TO GOD

*I*N ELEMENTARY SCHOOL, my friends all played basketball in the Boys Club league. My friend Alan was one of those would-be, hardtop gladiators. The truth was he was a good basketball player, so when he entered class one morning with a huge cast, everyone wondered what had happened to him. This cast was not the run of the mill kind. It had a stabilizer bar and was obviously heavy. At lunch that day, we gathered around to hear Alan's tale of how all of this happened. His team was scrimmaging at practice.

The ball was going out of bounds when Alan tried to knock the ball back into play. While he successfully got the ball back in bounds, he used his hand to stop himself from hitting a wall. What resulted was a compound break. When he made it to the emergency room the doctor told Alan that he was about to experience the most painful thing he had ever experienced. The doctor was about to 'reconcile his bone structure'.

Reconciliation means to make straight or bring into harmony. Through the cross, Jesus painfully, at His own expense, reconciled us to God. He gave us the opportunity to have a relationship with His Father. Further, he brought about our reconciliation while we were still enemies of God.

As those who have been reconciled to God, we must bring reconciliation between God and others. 2 Corinthians 5:20 says, "Therefore we are ambassadors for Christ, as though God were making His appeal through us. We implore you on behalf of Christ: Be reconciled to God." Ambassadors stand for the interests of and speak on behalf of another. As Christians, we stand for God's interests and have the privilege to speak on his behalf with the Good News of the Gospel, which brings reconciliation to all who believe.

<u>Reflections</u>

When were you reconciled to God?

Do you see yourself as an ambassador for Christ? Why or Why not?

Do people around you know you're an ambassador for Christ?

Cleanse out the old leaven that you may be a new lump, as you really are unleavened. For Christ, our Passover lamb has been sacrificed.

1 Corinthians 5:7

"The most obscene symbol in human history is the Cross; yet in its ugliness it remains the most eloquent testimony to human dignity"

R.C. Sproul

NEW PASSOVER
LAMB

*I*MAGINE, JESUS IS with His disciples at the annual Passover Meal. It had been an unusual week. Earlier in the week, Jesus was celebrated by the people, who welcomed Him with palm branches and saying "Hosanna!" Over the next few days, He preaches some of His final messages, spends time with some of his closest friends and overturns the tables in the Temple. It had been a busy week. Now, it is Thursday evening. He is with His disciples, who have no clue as to what will happen next.

The Passover was given to the people of Israel,

during the time of Moses. Jesus and disciples were simply remembering this event in the way Moses had told them to. For centuries, Jews, like Jesus and His disciples had taken part in this meal. The people of God had been prisoners under Egyptian oppression for over four centuries. God heard their cry for freedom. He sent Moses to Pharaoh to broker the Hebrew people's release. The pharaoh was hard of heart. He would not release them. So, God sent a series of plagues, culminating in the Death Angel. The Death Angel was to kill the firstborn of every home that did not have the blood of a Passover Lamb over its door post. That night, terror broke out in Egypt, as the shrieks of parents could be heard, as they discovered their lifeless children. Yet, in the Hebrew homes, where the blood of a lamb was applied to the doorpost, no one was harmed.

Following the traditional Passover meal, Jesus took this tradition and deepened it. He took bread, unleavened bread, and broke it. He then told each disciple too, "Take, eat. This is my body." Then, he took the Passover wine and he compared it to His blood. He told them to "Drink it." Jesus was showing His disciples Himself in the Passover Feast. It is Jesus' blood, when applied to the doorpost of our lives, spares us from eternal death. Romans 8:2 says, "For the law of the Spirit of life has set you free in Christ Jesus from the law of sin and death."

Reflections

How does it feel to know you will live forever?

Where does the 'blood of Christ' need to still be applied in your life?

In my Father's house are many rooms. If it were not so, would I have told you that I go to prepare a place for you? And if I go and prepare a place for you, I will come again and will take you to myself, that where I am you may be also.

John 14:2-3

Life, if properly viewed in any aspect, is great, but mainly great when viewed in its relation to the world to come"

Albert Barnes

Yes, we are of good courage, and we would rather be away from the body and at home with the Lord.

2 Corinthians 5:8

DEATH IS NOT THE END

*I*N THIS VERSE, Jesus talks about after the cross, His resurrection, and ascension back to Heaven. That He prepares a place for us with the Father. Specifically, He says we get a room in the 'Father's house'. Years ago, I was in the United Kingdom on a city tour. As we drove, on our double-decker, red bus through the narrow streets, the guide pointed to several buildings and said, "You will notice the mansions on each side." He was pointing to apartments. At the end of our tour, I asked him why he called apartments, mansions. He referred to the verse above and he said, "Don't you remember in the King James Version of it says, 'In my Father's house are many mansions'?"

I grew up thinking, most of my Christian life, that when I died I would get a large mansion in Heaven. I used to watch an old TV show called the *Beverly Hillbillies.* I grew up believing a mansion was something like one might find in Beverly Hills, CA. So, I thought I would get a big house and swimming pool on a palatial estate. So, my British guide really enhanced my understanding of Heaven that day.

A 'mansion' in the KJV was an apartment; a room, among many, under one single roof. In the Jewish culture, a young man would take his bride to the bridal chamber, which was a room added on to his father's house. The Church is the bride of Christ. The imagery here is beautiful. As individuals, being part of the Bride of Christ, means that when we die, we move into the Father's House. Christ takes us into His home.

Many times, a believer's final moment is their hardest moment. I have been at the bedside of many

Christ-followers, who took their last breath at home, a nursing home or hospital, racked with pain. Yet, on the other side of their hardest moment was their best moment—Heaven.

<u>Reflections</u>

What will your moment right after your 'hardest moment' be like?

How does it feel to know that life is not over when you leave this earth?

Knowing that there is life after this time on earth, what needs to change in your life?

But he was pierced for our transgressions; he was crushed for our iniquities; upon him was the chastisement that brought us peace, and with his wounds we are healed.

Isaiah 53:5

"God will remove the sources of sorrow--- "death or mourning or crying or pain." There will be everlasting joy and bliss, for the debilitating effects of sin and suffering have been taken away."

Grant Osborne

DEATH AND DISEASE DEFEATED

I *LOST MY* Dad to the enemy of death and disease on October 16, 2017. To that point in life I had never lost anyone that close to me. I saw his life slowly ebb away for nearly a decade from a terrible disease. Death and disease are enemies, no matter how we try to explain them away.

In the creation story, God says, "…it was very good." In the beginning God created everything perfect. There was no sickness, disease, or death. humanity and creation were perfect. When sin entered the world, it was a death sentence to man. James 1:15 says, "Then desire when it has conceived gives birth to sin, and sin when it is fully grown, brings forth death." This death is first in the body. Unless Christ returns, everyone on planet earth will experience bodily death. But sin, also brings death spiritually. Jesus told a man named Nicodemus, "Truly, truly, I say to you, unless one is born again he cannot see the kingdom of God. (John 3:3)" This simply means that if you are born once you will die twice. This means that you will be born physically and then die physically and die spiritually in a place called Hell. Yet, if you are born twice, you will experience physical birth, then physical death, only to be birthed into Heaven.

You see, the process of physical death is always a result of sin, through the pain of debilitating and failing bodies. Ezekiel 18:4 says, "…the soul who sins shall die." Every cancer, each accident, heart attacks, diabetes, you name it is a result of sin.

Yet in the verse above we see that Christ's physical death has liberated our physical bodies. Jesus in His earthly ministry healed countless people. He still does and can, but sometimes He does not. One thing is for certain, He heals Christ-followers 100% of the time, sometimes here and sometimes hereafter. Revelation 21:4 says, "He will wipe away every tear from their eyes, and death shall be no more, neither shall there be mourning, nor crying, nor pain anymore, for the former things have passed away." There is hope everlasting in Christ, rest in this hope.

Reflections

Have you ever known someone who was healed?

How do you respond to death considering the Cross?

How does the truth, "Death shall be no more" encourage you today?

And if you call on him as Father who judges impartially according to each one's deeds, conduct yourselves with fear throughout the time of your exile, knowing that you were ransomed from the futile ways inherited from your forefathers, not with perishable things such as silver or gold, but with the precious blood of Christ, like that of a lamb without blemish or spot.

1 Peter 1:17-19

"I thought I could leap from earth to heaven at one spring when I first saw my sins drowned in the Redeemer's blood."

Charles Spurgeon

FREEDOM FROM PASSED DOWN SIN

I *HAVE KNOWN* many people who fall into the trap of believing in generational bondage. It is true that some cultures, peoples, and families have some distinctive sins. Like me, you have known families that the various generations have had a struggle with the same sin. Whether it be alcoholism, abuse, divorce, immorality, or any number of vices Christ has set us free from our lineage.

1 Peter 1 says we were 'ransomed from the futile

ways inherited from your forefathers'. And, how did this ransom occur? It happened through the 'precious blood of Christ'. The saving power is in proportion to the Savior. Christ breaks the chain of sin. Only Christ's blood is enough to free us from any form of vice. You do not have to be the sinful generations before you. In fact, the power to break the cyclical nature of generational sin is available to you. Ezekiel 18:20 says it like this, "The soul who sins shall die. The son shall not suffer for the iniquity of the father, nor the father suffers for the iniquity of the son..." We can be influenced by our ancestors, but we are not bound to their sinful patterns.

What was not enough to break the curse was 'with perishable things such as silver or gold'. Silver and gold represent the things we use to try to bring about our own liberation. I wonder how much money is spent on counselors, therapists, medicines to 'fix' ourselves. There is no doubt, these things are all valid and good when properly understood. Yet, most of our problems can be fixed by simply appropriating the gift of Christ's blood, from His cross, over the 'issues' of our lives.

Reflections

What generational sin do you need to be free from?

How can you be the catalyst for change in generations
to come?

What would it take for you to walk in freedom today?

Whoever makes a practice of sinning is of the devil, for the devil has been sinning from the beginning. The reason the Son of God appeared was to destroy the works of the devil. No one born of God makes a practice of sinning, for God's seed abides in him; and he cannot keep on sinning, because he has been born of God.

1 John 3:8-9

"Christ in you, the hope of glory," I'm not afraid of the devil. The devil can handle me—he's got judo I never heard of. But he can't handle the One to whom I'm joined; he can't handle the One to whom I'm united; he can't handle the One whose nature dwells in my nature."

A.W. Tozer

IT DESTROYS
SATAN.

SATAN IS A defeated foe. His rebellion began in Heaven, where he was an angel. In fact, he led worship there. Isaiah 14:12-15 speaks of his fall when it says, "How you are fallen from heaven, O Lucifer, son of the morning! How you are cut down to the ground, you who weakened the nations! For you have said in your heart: 'I will ascend into heaven, I will exalt my throne above the stars of God; I will also sit on the mount of the congregation in the farthest sides of the north; I will ascend above the heights of the clouds, I will be like the Highest.' Yet you shall be brought down to Sheol, To the lowest depths of the Pit." He wanted to be God.

God is so incredibly gracious to us. Think about it. He will share his Son, Jesus, with us. He will share Heaven with us. He will give us 'all things that pertain to life and godliness'. He denies us no good gifts. He loves us with an 'everlasting love' (Jer. 31:3). He has gifted us each with different abilties. (Eph. 4:7). He has things that only you can do (Eph. 2:8). But, there is one thing that God will not share with us—His Glory! Isaiah 42:8 says, "I am the LORD; that is my name; my glory I give to no other, nor my praise to carved idols."

Man, just like Satan, has always wanted God's glory. This is why the serpent, Satan, in the Garden of Eden, says to Eve, "For God knows that when you eat of it your eyes will be opened, and you will be like God, knowing good and evil." (Gen. 3:5). The sin of both man and Satan is wanting to be God--pride. But, as the verse above says, Christ appears in the flesh, goes to cross, to destroy the works of Satan. Therefore, the grip of sin is no longer mandated for people. So, let us not let the defeated foe, whose destiny is the lake of fire (Rev. 20:10), take us or others with him.

Reflections

How does it feel to know that Satan is defeated?

How can you live each day in this victory?

What areas do you let Satan defeat you in?

How can you live each day in the victory the Cross ushers in to those who believe?

When Jesus had received the sour wine, he said, "It is finished," and he bowed his head and gave up his spirit.

John 19:30

"Of the Cross of Christ is anything to the mind, it is surely everything—the most profound reality and the sublimest mystery."

John Stott

IT FINISHES 'IT'

IN HUMAN HISTORY there have been some incredible battle cries that have rallied armies and people. Being a native Texan, one battle cry that Texans take great pride in is, "Remember the Alamo!" After the Texas forces were obliterated by the Mexican Army this battle cry propelled Sam Houston's army to victory. Or, the cry of every good US Marine is "Oorah!" It has been the go-to for every Leatherneck since Vietnam.

Yet the greatest battle cry ever uttered into sound, occurred from the cross of Jesus when He said, "It is finished!" The battle lines were drawn hundreds of years before the cross. The conflict began in a garden, The Garden of Eden, when Satan, disguised as a serpent, led mankind, through Adam and Eve, into sin. In Genesis 3:15, "…he shall bruise your head, and you shall bruise his heel", a veiled reference to when God would defeat Satan through Jesus, the Messiah.

Throughout the ages, Satan tried his best to thwart the plan of God of liberating mankind from sin. He attempted to destroy the promised Messiah. In Egypt, where the Israelites were enslaved for 400 years, he attempted to destroy the Savior by having pharaoh kill all the Hebrew babies, yet Moses was spared. Then, Satan tried it again, by having Herod kill all the boys 2 years of age and younger. But, through a dream, God warned Joseph to take Jesus to Egypt, of all places, to escape the slaughter. Satan had worked throughout history trying to destroy Jesus before Jesus could destroy him. Yet, with all that effort, it did not work.

When Jesus spread his arms out on the cross and said, "It is finished!" He was saying, "It was finished. It was accomplished. It is over." Satan no longer held humanity captive to sin. The bond of sin was broken in

Christ's work. The Apostle Paul said it like this, "For God has done what the law, weakened by the flesh, could not do. By sending his own Son in the likeness of sinful flesh and for sin, he condemned sin in the flesh, in order that the righteous requirement of the law might be fulfilled in us, who walk not according to the flesh but according to the Spirit." (Romans 8:3)

<u>Reflections</u>

Knowing, "It is finished!" What still needs to be finished in your life?

What is your battle cry today, in light of what Christ has done for you?

For the love of Christ controls us, because we have concluded this: that one has died for all, therefore all have died; and he died for all, that those who live might no longer live for themselves but for him who for their sake died and was raised.

2 Corinthians 5:14-15

"Pride must die in you, or nothing of heaven can live in you"

Andrew Murray

FREEDOM FOR ME

*T*HE MOST PLEASING sound to the human ear is the sound of their own name. We love to hear our name spoken. In fact, a love of self will motivate a lot of our decision making. When I was in the 7th grade, I quit the football team. I just didn't like it. It was hard, hot and I had to stay after school too long. Football cut into my needed 'down time'. Yet, as the season went on, I kept hearing the names of my friends being acknowledged for their tackles and touchdowns on the morning announcements. It made me disgruntled. I thought to myself many times, "I could do that. I am faster than that guy." The next season, I played 8th-grade football and continued through high school. The pride of self of awareness will cause you to do many things.

Pride is the sin of every other sin. Pride is self-worship. Everyone in Hell is there ultimately because of pride. It can be summed up in the lie that the Serpent told Adam and Eve, in Genesis 3:5, "For God knows that when you eat of it your eyes will be opened, and you will be like God, knowing good and evil." Pride essentially wants to be like God. Prideful people want glory, recognition, freedom, autonomy, etc.

In the verse above, we are reminded that the cross gives us the ability to become Christ-followers, we died with Jesus and he died so that people would be free of themselves. Christianity is a life for life exchange. Christ gives His life for our salvation. We aren't our own anymore. Therefore, if we are truly saved, we give Him all our lives. The secret to battling the sin of pride in our lives is a continual dying to self. John Owen, a Puritan pastor, said it best, "Be killing sin or sin be killing you."

Reflections

How has pride affected your relationships and your influence?

What sin needs to be killed in you? Will you surrender it to Jesus?

You are not your own, for you were bought with a price. So, glorify God in your body.

1 Corinthians 6:19b-20

"God exchanged his own Son for you! The Cross proves your value. Jesus didn't die for junk. You are incredibly valuable. Nobody has ever paid a greater price than God for you. You are acceptable and you are valuable."

Rick Warren

GIVES ME VALUE

*O*NE OF THE constant problems that seem to plague people is low self-esteem. It doesn't matter if you are a younger person or older person, the struggle is real when it comes to this issue. It is ironic that young people have struggled with low self-image, given that the current generation's parents have tried hard to combat this phenomenon. It is hard to believe that older people struggle with this, but the truth is Senior adults can have the same insecurities that millennials do.

Low self-esteem can have many effects, but the

greatest one is to live below your value. When Christ died for you, He set your value. What did Jesus use to set your value? His own blood. Acts 20:28 says, "...care for the church of God, which he obtained with his own blood." On the cross there came a point when Roman soldiers punctured His side to expedite his death because the Jewish Passover demanded the crucifixion be finished by sundown. John 19:34 says, "But one of the soldiers pierced his side with a spear, and at once there came out blood and water." What is certain is that Christ's blood, all His blood, was used to purchase you.

Therefore, live to your value. Use your body to glorify the Lord in all things. When you consider an activity, ask yourself, "Does this activity cause me to live to my value?" When you think about entering a relationship, ask yourself, "Does this relationship allow me to live to my value? Does it cause me to do things that value me or devalue me?" In your occupation, ask yourself, "Can I live to my value doing this?" When Christ sets your value never let anyone lower it. You are of infinite worth because He extravagantly set your price.

<u>Reflections</u>

What has low self-esteem caused you to do?

How does it feel to know you have had a high price paid for you?

How does knowing Jesus paid His life for you change the way you see yourself? How can you live in this truth today?

"This is my commandment, that you love one another as I have loved you. Greater love has no one than this, that someone lay down his life for his friends. You are my friends if you do what I command you. No longer do I call you servants, for the servant does not know what his master is doing; but I have called you friends, for all that I have heard from my Father I have made known to you."

John 15:12-15

"The dearest friend on earth is a mere shadow compared to Jesus Christ."

Oswald Chambers

FRIENDSHIP WITH GOD

WE ARE ALL born into families, but we choose our friends. It has been said that "Blood is thicker than water", meaning that family bonds are greater than all other bonds. Without a doubt, there is some truth to that statement. However, many family bonds are motivated by obligation. Parents have a responsibility to take care of children. In turn, children will one day take responsibility for their parents. Spouses are obligated to love and serve one another. Marriages are covenants, sealed before God, Himself. Brothers look after brothers and sisters are to be each other's keeper.

However, friendships are optional and discretionary. C.S. Lewis said it best, "Friendship is unnecessary, like philosophy, like art... It has no survival value; rather it is one of those things which give value to survival." Friends make life worth living and they are God's gift to us in helping us grow as individuals.

Therefore, it is so revolutionary that Jesus would call his followers friends. As we choose friends, Jesus chooses His friends. How humbling it is to know that He calls Christ-followers friends. If you are a Christ-follower, He calls you a friend.

And, like a good friend, He meets a need in your life that you cannot meet on your own. Great friends extrapolate from your flaws you do not see in yourself. Jesus saw beyond the scars and ugliness of our sins. He knew the masterpiece that is you behind the veil of sin. Therefore, He dies on the cross to rescue you from your sin so that you can become the authentic you that He created you to be. What a friend we have in Jesus.

<u>Reflections</u>

Who is your best friend?

How does it feel to know Christ wants to be your friend?

The best way to grow a friendship is to spend time with one another, How can you spend more time with Christ each day?

"And they sang a new song, saying, "Worthy are you to take the scroll and to open its seals, for you were slain, and by your blood, you ransomed people for God from every tribe and language and people and nation..."

Revelation 5:9

"Our lives begin to end the day we become silent about things that matter"

Martin Luther King Jr.

IT ENDS RACISM

ON APRIL 4, 1968, in Memphis, Tennessee at 6 P.M., a sniper's bullet struck, and eventually, killed Martin Luther King Jr. King Jr. had been a leader of the U.S. Civil Rights movement for over 20 years. He was a proponent of non-violent protests in response to segregation and racial inequality. His most famous speech was entitled, "I Have a Dream" given on the steps of the Lincoln Memorial on August 28, 1963. In the speech, he says, "I have a dream that my four little children will one day live in a nation where they will not be judged by the color of their skin, but by the content of their character."

Today, as in the days gone by, racial reconciliation continues to be difficult. Racial tension is not something that isolated to one country in the world. It is a global problem. In the West, the Middle East, and Asia, where there are differences in people, there will be racism. One group will always claim superiority over another.

Yet, in the person of Christ, and only through Him, is there hope. In the verse above, it says that Jesus died for every people, of every tribe, nation, and tongue. Galatians 3:28 says, "There is neither Jew nor Greek, there is neither slave nor free, there is no male and female, for you are all one in Christ Jesus." For the world to reconcile racially, the races must find their origin in a common person—Jesus. When Christ went to the cross, all nations and peoples were bought by His blood. Therefore, all people, who call upon the name of the Lord and are saved, are now connected to His blood. We are all now family by His blood. One day we will all be in Heaven together and it will not be segregated. The greatest witness we can have to the world is to break racial barriers among Jesus's family.

Reflections

Do you have deep relationships with people who do not look like you?

Can you imagine what Heaven will be like with all the tribes and tongues together?

How should the imagine of Heaven being filled with every tribe and tongues affect your interactions with people who do not look or talk like you?

For I have come down from heaven, not to do my own will but the will of him who sent me.

John 6:38

And walk in love, as Christ loved us and gave himself up for us, a fragrant offering and sacrifice to God.

Ephesians 5:2

"God is the archetypal Father; all other fatherhood is a more or less imperfect copy of his pefect fatherhood"

F.F. Bruce

IT PLEASED HIS FATHER

*I*HAD THE greatest Dad ever. He constantly bombarded me with love and affection. I received text messages that always affirmed me, even when I knew my performance was less than stellar. I had a good relationship with my Father at every stage of life. He loved me unconditionally and I can say I always wanted to please him.

Sadly, many people have a broken lens about God because they have a broken lens about their earthly fathers. Earthly fathers help children know what God is really like. When an earthly father loves his children unconditionally, they have a real sense of the heart of God. Yet, when a father is critical, harsh, withholds love or is abusive, the lens of fatherhood is cracked. The Devil is smart. He knows that if he can crack the lens of fatherhood, in a person, he can make it difficult for them to relate to God as the Father.

Yet, Christ's sacrifice proves the kind of father the Heavenly Father is. Christ's Father, the Heavenly Father, is so good that He wanted to please Him. Jesus wanted to honor his Father by doing the most difficult thing imaginable, dying on the cross. Jesus did the Fathers will, but He was not forced to do it. John 18:10 says, "No one takes it from me, but I lay it down of my own accord. I have authority to lay it down, and I have authority to take it up again. This charge I have received from my Father."

Jesus submitted to the Father's plan because He knew it was a good plan because He is a good Father. He could be trusted. May we fathers demonstrate this goodness to our own children, so that they may know our good Father.

<u>Reflections</u>

How has your relationship with your father affected your relationship with your Heavenly Father?

Do you believe that God is a good Father, who has your best interests in mind? If not, why?

For he who was called in the Lord as a bondservant is a freedman of the Lord. Likewise, he who was free when called is a bondservant of Christ. You were bought with a price; do not become bondservants of men.

1 Corinthians 7:22-23

"He is no fool who gives what he cannot keep, to gain what he cannot lose."

Jim Elliot

SHOWS OUR UTILITY

*O*N NOVEMBER 15, 2017, Leonardo da Vinci's Salvator Mundi (Savior of the World) sold for $450 million dollars, making it the most expensive painting ever sold. Saudi prince Bader bin Abullah bin Mohammed Farhan al-Saud bought it. What is interesting about the painting is that some art experts are not sure it really is a Da Vinci painting at all. Yet, the Prince paid a high price for this unique work of art.

Now, I doubt I will ever be able to see this priceless piece of art in the Prince's home, but I bet he has it on display in a grand way. However, the Prince can choose to do with the painting what He chooses to do. If he wants the painting on display publicly, he can do so. If he would like to have the painting locked in a closet out of sight, that is his choice. Why? He owns the painting.

In the same sense, Christ's death on the cross bought us as his very own. We belong to him. Paul used the term 'bondservant' meaning one bound for life. In ancient times, there were two kinds of servants. There were voluntary, servants who would work for a master until a debt was paid off. Then, there were bondservants, who would work for a master their entire life because the master paid for them.

Just as the Saudi Prince owns Da Vinci's painting so Christ owns you because of the price He paid for you on the cross. This is a tough concept for Westerners who have fought against slavery and value individual freedom. Yet, there is great freedom found in being Christ's bondservant. Servants simply live at the pleasure of their masters. As Christ-followers, we simply live at the pleasure of Jesus. We go where he tells us to go. We say what he tells us to say. We do what he tells us to do. There is great freedom in this reality. Being Christ's servants means that we do not have to worry about the greatness or smallness of our lives, only our faithfulness to Him.

Reflections

How does it feel to be free from the bondage of sin, but a bondservant to Christ?

What does it look like to live at the pleasure of your master today?

Likewise, my brothers, you also have died to the law through the body of Christ, so that you may belong to another, to him who has been raised from the dead, in order that we may bear fruit for God.

Romans 7:4

"Have you ever noticed how much of Christ's life was spent doing kind things?"

Henry Drummond

SO, WE CAN BEAR FRUIT

*A*CCORDING TO ROMANS, chapter seven verse four when Christ died we died with him to the law. The law is what brought about our death sentence. We were not able to keep the law and we sinned. One of my friends who is in law enforcement says, "The wheels of justice turn slowly and grind finely." Apart from Christ, we would suffer under the severity of the punishment of the law. But, because we died with Christ, God sees us as one of his own.

Jesus did this so that our lives could be 'fruitful'. One of the ways a believer can confirm their profession as a Christian is that their life bears fruit. The trouble is we sometimes confuse fruit with worldly success. You can be a pastor who is successful and not fruitful. God is not judging our lives by our successes, but by our fruit. 1 Samuel 16:7 says, "...For the Lord sees not as man sees: man looks on the outward appearance, but the Lord looks on the heart." What does fruit look like?

First, fruit is expected. John 15:16 says, "You did not choose me, but I chose you and appointed you that you should go and bear fruit and that your fruit should abide..." Jesus cannot imagine a non-fruit bearing Christian.

Next, fruit should 'abide'. Eternal fruit lasts. While the action or word is done in a moment, the effect is eternal. It changes lives here on the earth and receives rewards there in Heaven.

Then, fruit is a product of the Holy Spirit. Galatians 5:22-23 says, "But the fruit of the Spirit is love, joy, peace, patience, kindness, goodness, faithfulness, gentleness, self-control; against such things, there is no law." The Holy Spirit causes fruit to be produced in you that would not have occurred on its own.

So, how 'fruity' are you? Every Christian, who is real, produces fruit. Some years our lives have lots of fruit. Other years not as much. The point is, in every year, it produces something. The cross creates for us the ability to bear fruit.

<u>Reflections</u>

Where are you bearing fruit? If nowhere, why is that?

Who do you know who is 'fruity'? Encourage them and tell them you see Jesus in them.

THE CROSS

Truly, truly, I say to you, unless a grain of wheat falls into the earth and dies, it remains alone; but if it dies, it bears much fruit.

John 12:24

"We must cease striving and trust God to provide what He thinks is best and in whatever time He chooses to make it available. But this kind of trusting doesn't come naturally. It's a spiritual crisis of the will in which we must choose to exercise faith"

Charles R. Swindoll

WE WILL REAP
WHAT WE SOW

WHEN A FARMER has a barren field, what does he do? He could complain about it. He could make excuses for it. He could pray about it. Yet, none of those things will help him until he plants a seed. He must get the seed in the ground to see the condition of the field change.

In the verse above, Jesus is saying, "I am going to die and go into the tomb. Later, I am going to break out of the ground, just like the seed breaks forth from the earth into something different than a seed. I am going to do this to ransom the souls of countless millions of people. My one life will be expended for the many."

Many times, we sit back and wait on God to do something about our situation. We want Him to act and right now! Yet, many times God is saying, "Plant a seed." Until we get the seed in the ground of our lives, our situations will never change

Sowing and reaping is a foundational concept to believers. We will always reap what we sow, later than we sow it and different than we sow it. You always have something to sow---a seed. Rick Warren says it like this, "When you have a need, plant a seed."

So, where do you need to plant some seeds? Think about it. If you need energy, you might need to spend some energy. Take care of your body. Do you need some romance in your marriage? You might need to sow the seeds that yield that response in your spouse. Do you need money? You should give away some money. This one might be the toughest one to wrap your mind around. Do you need encouragement? If your words encourage others, it is amazing how you will receive what you need.

In every need that we plant a seed, we exercise faith. Faith always moves God—it moves Him to act. It is faith that motivates God. (Hebrews 11:6). Just as Jesus, practiced selfless faith and millions of people have been saved, our seeds of faith ought to bless others and become our legacy.

Reflections

Where do you need to plant seeds for your needs?

In what ways is your life selfless?

How have you excersied faith this last week?

Therefore, since we are surrounded by so great a cloud of witnesses, let us also lay aside every weight, and sin which clings so closely, and let us run with endurance the race that is set before us, looking to Jesus, the founder and perfecter of our faith, who for the joy that was set before him endured the cross, despising the shame, and is seated at the right hand of the throne of God.

Hebrews 12:1-2

"But Resurrection is not just consolation—it is restoration. We get it all back—the love, the loved ones, the goods, the beauties of this life—but in new, unimaginable degrees of glory and joy and strength."

Tim Keller

DELAYED JOY

*C*RUCIFIXION MIGHT BE the worst form of torture to ever be dreamed up in the imagination of deranged men. The process was slow and agonizing. It was intended to squeeze every ounce of life out of its participant and maximize each painful moment. Agony, through the crucifixion, was slow and calculated.

After a victim had been tortured, usually through flogging, they were forced to carry their own cross beam, known as the pitabulum, to the site of the execution. The pitabulum usually weighed between 75 to 125 pounds.

THE CROSS

The journey was usually about one mile over uneven terrain. Once at the execution site, the crucified one's wrists were nailed to the pitabulum, between the radius and the ulna. If the spike had been driven into the hands, as traditionally pictured, the weight of the victim would rip through the hands. Then, a large spike was driven through the tops of the feet into the vertical beam. This was done to give the victim leverage to breathe. He would push up against the spike to open the lungs enough to grasp for air. Crucifixion was suffocating. Then, the vertical beam was then raised and dropped into a hole. The victim would cry out in pain, as the beam landed in the hole. Their fresh nail wounds would agitate with the violent jostle. Death would still be hours away unless, in the case of Jesus, it is sped up. Most of the time, death took hours and days. Victims died from loss of blood, asphyxiation, and dehydration.

Yet, Jesus did all of this because of delayed gratification. He knew that after the cross, He would experience the joy of being reunited with His Father. He would once again take back his spot in Heaven. Momentary suffering was worth the joy of eternity. Jesus knew that the pain was worth the pleasure to come. What about you? We live in an on-demand world. Most of the time we want what we want and we want it now. Yet, the best things and the highest joys must be deferred—in our relationships, in our money, in our lives and certainly in our eternities.

Reflections

What have you delayed your gratification for?

Refect on one time you went through suffering that was worth it? How sweet was the delayed gradifiction?

Is Christ worth 'momentary suffering'?

Then he said to them, "My soul is very sorrowful, even to death; remain here, and watch with me." And going a little farther he fell on his face and prayed, saying, "My Father, if it be possible, let this cup pass from me; nevertheless, not as I will, but as you will."

Matthew 26:38-39

"By perseverance the snail reached the ark"

Charles Spurgeon

PERSEVERANCE
THROUGH PAIN

WHEN YOU REFLECT on the happenings on the cross, some 2,000 years ago, it's hard to believe that there was any joy there. Where was the joy in watching a man, Jesus, who had been sleeping deprived, tortured, beaten, mocked, framed by religious officials, forsaken by his friends, bleed out on a device that was the cruelest instrument of death imaginable…the cross? Where is the joy in recalling how he died between thieves, like a common criminal? Where is the joy in remembering his mother was at the foot of the cross, watching these events play out? You can only imagine how her heart must have broken, as she remembered your little baby, now far removed from Bethlehem's stable. Where was the joy in any of this?

We are reminded today, that the joy Jesus was to experience was after the cross. Jesus knew the pain he was to endure through his crucifixion. Therefore, in the Garden of Gethsemane, he pleaded with the Father on three occasions, "to let this cup pass". Yet, it was God's will for Him to endure momentary pain so He could experience eternal pleasure.

This is true for believers. We are going to experience the pain of all varieties in this world. We must remember that "For this light momentary affliction is preparing for us an eternal weight of glory beyond all comparison..." (2 Corinthians 4:17) The reality is, that for most of us, our last moments will be our toughest moments. I have seen this play out repeatedly in the lives of believers who are about to be promoted to Heaven. Most of the time, their last moments are difficult. Sometimes their last season in life is tough. Yet, right behind a believer's toughest moment lies their greatest moment, as they push off this mortal frame and step into the eternal. Knowing what is behind our most difficult times in life allows us to bear whatever we are experiencing. For, one day we will be with Him, in Heaven.

Reflections

What is the toughest thing you have endured?

How does the cross bring joy to pain?

How does grace help you cope with struggles?

"...this Jesus delivered up according to the definite plan and foreknowledge of God, you crucified and killed by the hands of lawless men."

Acts 2:23

"In God's hands intended evil becomes eventual good."

Max Lucado

TO GIVE US GOOD NEWS

***W*E LIVE IN** a world that gives very little good news. If you turn on the television, open a newspaper or look at an internet feed, you will find that most of the news is depressing, negative and hostile. In fact, our world suffers from 'compassion fatigue'. Compassion fatigue is a result of a news cycle that never stops and is always trying to sensationalize what is new. Compassion fatigue happens slowly over time.

In the same way, most people reading this live in the United States of America. We have a rich Christian heritage. As I write this I live in Dallas/Fort Worth. In our area, we have some of the largest churches in the country. In a radius of 30 miles, you can see some of the best preachers, hear the greatest music and enjoy multimillion-dollar, state of the art facilities. Yet, most of the metroplex is without Jesus.

The combination of compassion fatigue and an oversaturation of the Gospel has turned the 'good news' into just news. 2 Corinthians 4:4 says it like this, "In their case the god of this world has blinded the minds of the unbelievers, to keep them from seeing the light of the gospel of the glory of Christ, who is the image of God." Satan has worked diligently to blind people from the truth of the Gospel. And it is not just Satan working against people, their own dead nature is at work as well, "The natural person does not accept the things of the Spirit of God, for they are folly to him, and he is not able to understand them because they are spiritually discerned" (1 Corinthians 2:14)

Therefore, when Christ died on the cross, the regenerative power of the Gospel became a possibility.

TO SHOW EVIL CAN BE USED FOR GOOD

ONE OF THE toughest questions that I ever get asked is, "Why do bad things happen to good people?" This question has disillusioned many people out of the faith. As a pastor, I have had to try to answer this question on some level many times. Whether it be a young person who dies in a car wreck, a baby who is stillborn, a mother who is taken from her young children, a disease, a divorce, or some other tragedy, how can God use this terrible situation for good is a constant theme.

One of the first realizations that people must come to grips with is that good and bad things happen to everyone. Matthew 5:45 says it like this, "...For he makes his sun rise on the evil and on the good, and sends rain on the just and on the unjust." What does this mean? Bad and good things happen to bad and good people in equal measure.

Next, the world is full of the pain and destruction because of sin. Sin has broken the world in all respects. It has broken our relationships with God and each other and the physical world itself. Therefore, bad things will happen in a broken world.

Then, in the verse above, we see that God allows some pain into our lives. Nothing happens that is not 'according to the definite plan and foreknowledge of God'. God allowed pain into his son's life. Therefore, some pain is coming into our lives.

Had God not allowed the death of His son, we would have no access to God. We would be eternally condemned and separated from Him forever. His death brings us life. God brings life to death. Like Joseph said to his brothers, after they sold him into slavery "You intended to harm me, but God intended it all for good. He brought me to this position so I could save the lives of many people." (Genesis 50:20) God brings good from bad.

Further, if we can really have 'heaven on earth', then why would we want to go to heaven? The pain of this world prepares us for the eternal pleasure of the other. 2 Peter 2:11 says, "Beloved, I urge you as sojourners and exiles to abstain from the passions of the flesh, which wage war against your soul." Pain, sin, death, and brokenness remind us that we are not home yet, while the Cross reminds us God will always make good come from Evil.

Reflections

How has God brought something good out of your greatest pain?

Where have you seen God move in a 'good way' in a bad situation?

For the word of the cross is folly to those who are perishing, but to us who are being saved it is the power of God.

1 Corinthians 1:18

"The Gospel is the good news that the everlasting and ever-increasing joy of the never-boring, ever-satisfying Christ is ours freely and eternally by faith in the sin-forgiving death and hope-giving resurrection of Jesus Christ."

John Piper

Romans 1:16 says, "For I am not ashamed of the gospel, for it is the power of God for salvation to everyone who believes, to the Jew first and to the Greek." If anyone can see the Gospel as accurate and correct, they need God to reveal it to them. This requires God to call them to Himself, "but to those who are called, both Jews and Greeks, Christ the power of God and the wisdom of God." (1 Corinthians 1:24) God must remove the Satanic roadblocks and the individuals own fleshly nature to reveal the Gospel or 'good news' to them. Therefore, when God calls a person, they must respond. He is under no obligation to do it again.

Reflections

Have you ever experienced compassion fatigue?

Has the Good news become news to you? Why?

THE CROSS

*Husbands, love your wives, as Christ loved the church
and gave himself up for her...*

Ephesians 5:25

*"Marriage was ordained for a remedy and to increase
the world and for the man to help the woman and the
woman the man, with all love and kindness"*

William Tyndale

MARRIAGE STANDARD SET

BEFORE THE INSTITUTION of the Church, or the government or any other man-made entity, God set up the marriage—between one man and one woman for one lifetime. The first wedding occurred in the Garden of Eden with Adam and Eve. Genesis 2:24 says, "Therefore a man shall leave his father and his mother and hold fast to his wife, and they shall become one flesh." On the cross, Christ deepened the meaning of marriage. In a day, when marriages break up at a rate of about 50%, traditional marriage has been redefined and younger generations are choosing cohabitation rather than to risk the potential pain of divorce, it is essential that we reclaim the primacy of marriage.

Why do marriages fail? There are many factors, at times it is communication, or intimacy, or infidelity. But, I would submit to you that most marriages fail due to a lack of love. When you consider the Church, remember that Jesus calls the Church His bride. Therefore, He is the groom. As husbands, we are not Jesus, but we are called to act like Him, with respect to our wives.

When you think about love what comes to mind? In our world, romantic love has gotten out of control. Frankly, many couples spend most of their engagement getting ready for the event, the actual wedding, and do not plan for the lifetime that follows behind it. Love is not always pampering and passionate. Christ's love is sacrificial.

Think about it. Christ gave Himself up so that His bride could experience the fullest of life. Why? Because He loved His bride, the Church. He did not expect the

Bride to sacrifice for Him. He sacrificed for her. What if husbands sacrificed regularly for their wives? Do you think homes, families, and marriages would be different? When wives feel loved, the way Christ loved, they will follow their husbands. This kind of love causes men not to use their strength for selfishness, but for selflessness. Our wives should able to reach things because of their husband's sacrifices that they could not achieve on their own.

Reflections

What is the difference between pampering and a sacrificial love?

If you are a husband, what has your wife achieved because of your sacrifice?

If you have a wife, how have you sacrificed for your husband?

What can you do today to show sacrificial love to your husband or wife?

"...who gave himself for us to redeem us from all lawlessness and to purify for himself a people for his own possession who are zealous for good works."

Titus 2:14

"the gospel also gives us new power for work by supplying us with a new passion and a deeper kind of rest."

Timothy Keller

FREEDOM TO WORK

ONE OF THE most liberating truths of the cross is how it changes our relationship with doing works or good deeds. When you consider the motivation of goods works, one must determine if these works are done out of relationship or religion. No doubt, our works are an outworking of our understanding of Jesus.

Some people fall into the trap of performing good works to earn their salvation. They believe that their right actions and good deeds will result in favor both here on earth and later in Heaven. The problem is our deeds are as filthy rags" (Is. 64:6). The Apostle Paul said it like this in Romans 8:3-4, "For God has done what the law, weakened by the flesh, could not do. By sending his own Son in the likeness of sinful flesh and for sin, he condemned sin in the flesh, in order that the righteous requirement of the law might be fulfilled in us, who walk not according to the flesh but according to the Spirit." We could not be good enough to earn our way to God. In fact, religion is dangerous because it attempts to put God in our debt through our behavior. God cares about the heart and this cannot be saved through religion.

Other people understand the power of relationship with God. We are not saved to God by our works, but so that we can work, like the verse above says, "zealous for good works". Ephesians 2:10 says it like this, "For we are his workmanship, created in Christ Jesus for good works, which God prepared beforehand, that we should walk in them." That word workmanship in the Greek means poem. God has put lots of creative thought into the lives of believers. He has things for them to do. Yet, for people in relationship with Jesus, they do 'good works' not to go to Heaven, but because they are going to Heaven.

Do our 'good works' matter? Absolutely, they do! But, a proper understanding of the motivation of those works is essential. Jesus did not die to create a religion for you, rather have a relationship with you. It is through the understanding of Jesus wanting a relationship with you so much that he died on a cross for you. That we are free to work with Jesus, not for salvation.

Reflections

When have you ever fallen prey to 'religion'?

How can you foster a deeper relationship with Christ?

God has works for you to do! What is keeping you from dong them?

But the free gift is not like the trespass. For if many died through one man's trespass, much more have the grace of God and the free gift by the grace of that one man Jesus Christ abounded for many. And the free gift is not like the result of that one man's sin. For the judgment following one trespass brought condemnation, but the free gift following many trespasses brought justification. For if, because of one man's trespass, death reigned through that one man, much more will those who receive the abundance of grace and the free gift of righteousness reign in life through the one man Jesus Christ. Therefore, as one trespass led to condemnation for all men, so one act of righteousness leads to justification and life for all men.

Romans 5:15-18

"Change always starts in your mind. The way you think determines the way you feel, and the way you feel influences the way you act"

Rick Warren

IT PUTS US IN THE RIGHT LINE

PROBABLY ONE OF the most aggravating activities anyone must endure is waiting in a line. If you are at all like me, you tend to 'wait in a hurry'. I don't like waiting at all. I remember a time when I was waiting in a very long line at a grocery store. Having read about half a tabloid magazine, which did you know that Elvis was abducted by aliens, I realized the holdup was the cashier. She was commenting one every product that every customer was buying. She gave her review of the product and was soliciting the opinions about other products she was not familiar with. As I inched up in line, I was getting more and more aggravated. In fact, I had made up my mind that as soon as I was at the front of the line, I was going to let this well intended lady know that her conversations were costing the rest of us precious time. As I made my way to the front, about to have my moment of truth, the cashier looked at me at said, "Pastor, good to see you! That was a great message last week," To which I said, "Thanks." I completely back pedaled on my bold intentions.

Everyone was born into a line. The line and lineage of Adam. He was the first man that God created. When he sinned, sin entered into mankind's bloodline. Just as we inherit physical characteristics from our parents, we inherit spiritual characteristics. We were born into sin. Psalm 51:5 says, "Behold, I was brought forth in iniquity, and in sin did my mother conceive me." In the bloodline of Adam, we are dead in our sins. We are in the executioner's line.

But, when Christ did His work on the cross, the opportunity to change lines became possible. We can now stand in the line that leads to life here and hereafter.

Reflections

When did you 'change lines' and trust Christ as your Savior? Have you done this yet?

What is the toughest thing about waiting?

Yet it was the will of the Lord to crush him; he has put him to grief; when his soul makes an offering for guilt, he shall see his offspring; he shall prolong his days;the will of the Lord shall prosper in his hand.Out of the anguish of his soul he shall see and be satisfied; by his knowledge shall the righteous one, my servant,make many to be accounted righteous, and he shall bear their iniquities.

Isaiah 53:10-11

"Redeeming sinners from all nations through Jesus Christ was God's plan from the beginning."

Colin Smith

WE SEE GOD'S PLAN

*W*HEN YOU THINK back to that hill called Golgotha, the place of the skull, and you consider Christ's crucifixion, you must ponder the question, "Who killed Jesus?" Was it Judas? Judas was one of his twelve disciples. He saw Jesus do everything from raise people from the dead, feed multitudes, walk on water and heal on command. Yet, Judas betrayed Jesus for 30 pieces of silver. But, while Judas was a traitor, he did not ultimately kill Jesus.

What about the Jewish leaders? Did they kill

Jesus? After all, they had worked for years to entrap Christ. They sought his death because they were jealous of his obvious power and influence with the people. He was a threat to their power. They led him, on the night before his crucifixion, through the kangaroo court which ultimately brought about his death. Yet, it was not the Jewish leaders who ultimately killed Jesus.

Could it have been Romans? They led out Christ's execution. It was Roman soldiers who scourged him, mocked him, beat him and ultimately murdered him. At any point, Pontius Pilate could have intervened and stopped the entire process, but he refused. In fact, Pilate washed his hands of Jesus.

Perhaps, it was the people who killed Jesus? If you remember, the same people who threw palm branches before him as he entered Jerusalem for the Passover on a donkey, were the same people who let a criminal go and insisted on Christ's death. But it was not the people who killed him.

No, the one behind the death of Christ was none other than God, the Father, himself. The only way for you and me to have righteousness before God was for Christ to die in our place. Righteousness means to have 'right standing'. The scripture says that our righteousness is as 'filthy rags'. Even at our best, it was not enough. We needed a Savior. We needed Christ to do for us what we could not do.

<u>Reflections</u>

How does it feel to know God had a plan from the beginning to save you?

Who in your life needs to know that God has a way fro them to receive salvation?

For we do not have a high priest who is unable to sympathize with our weaknesses, but one who in every respect has been tempted as we are, yet without sin.

Hebrews 4:15

Since we are members of his mystical body, we are united with him, and he is concerned with our troubles. From his own heart and affections, he gives us help and relief as is necessary. He is inwardly moved during our sufferings and trails with a sense of empathy.

John Owen

SYMPATHY SHOWN

FROM THE GARDEN of Eden until now, every person deals with temptation. Temptation is an interesting thing. It is similar, yet different for everyone. Temptation is a daily battle that everyone on the face of earth battles differently. The commonality of temptation is in its origin.

Temptations are found in three specific areas—the world, the flesh, and the Devil. Ephesians 2:2-3 says, "And you were dead in the trespasses and sins in which you once walked, following the course of this world, following the prince of the power of the air, the spirit that is now at work in the sons of disobedience— among whom we all once lived in the passions of our flesh, carrying out the desires of the body."

"The course of this world", refers to the cultural rejection of God. In our world today, people readily go against the plan and purpose of God. Selfishness, materialism, consumerism, and autonomy rule the day. The world continues to appeal to the parts of us that have not been fully surrendered to Christ.

"We all once lived in the passions of our flesh", is not referring to the actual physical body. God made all things, including our bodies. It is referring to our fallen nature, which Christ has subdued. The trouble is until we are made perfect in eternity, we will struggle with our flesh.

"Prince of the power of the air", refers to Satan and his demonic forces. Satan and his forces create issues in the world and in the Church. Just as Jesus experienced, both Satan and his demons, these forces can get personal with us.

The good news today is that Christ has overcome these areas. As the verse above states, He sympathizes with our weakness. In every way that we are, Jesus was tempted. Some might say, "Well it wasn't the same He was God." We must always remember that Jesus was fully God and fully man. He subjugated His deity so that He might identify with our humanity. Our confidence is this, "Yet in all these things we are more than conquerors through Him who loved us" (Romans 8:37). Therefore, walk in this confidence, you will fail, but know you have a Savior who sympathizes with your weakness. Run to Him, not from Him.

Reflections

Which area—the world, the flesh, or the devil—gives you the greatest struggle?

Do you have accountability in that area?

\

Since, therefore, we have now been justified by his blood, much more shall we be saved by him from the wrath of God.

Romans 5:9

To be justified means more than to be declared "not guilty." It actually means to be declared righteous before God. It means God has imputed or charged the gulit of our sin to His Son, Jesus Christ, and has imputed or credited Christ's righteousness to us.

Jerry Bridges

JUSTIFICATION PROVIDED

THROUGHOUT MY LIFE, I have always been intrigued by lawyers. I have had friends who have been attorneys and to hear them speak is interesting. One man shared with me that he represented some of the worst people in our city, who he knew committed horrible crimes. I asked him why he would willingly represent such people and attempt to lessen their crimes. He simply said,

"Everyone deserves their day in court." He was right, everyone will have their day in court.

It is great to be forgiven, but it is even better to be justified. In a human court, justification is a legal verdict. One is pronounced 'Just', meaning they have done everything correctly, properly or right. Justification is different than forgiveness. Forgiveness means that one admits to doing wrong, breaking the law or not being right. So, forgiveness and justification are two completely different concepts.

When a person's moral character changes after they receive Christ as their Savior and Lord, that act is called sanctification. Sanctification is the process of becoming more Christ-like throughout our lifetime. Our sanctification will ultimately lead to our glorification, when we move into eternity with Christ.

What is so amazing about justification is the fact that God, when He sees me, sees Christ's credited sacrifice over my life, and sees me as perfect. Think of it like this, the U2 front man, Bono, has an eye condition that forces him to wear eyeglasses all the time. Many times, he wears a rose or red tinted glass. When he looks at the world it is tinted. In the same way, when God, the

Father, looks upon your life, he looks through the rose-tinted glasses of Christ's blood and sees you not only as forgiven, but without any blemish. Perfect. Completely Justified.

Reflections

How does it feel to know you have been freely Justified?

Do we adequately see ourselves and others justified? If not, why?

What area in your life do you need to remind yourself you have been Justified?

How much more will the blood of Christ, who through the eternal Spirit offered himself without blemish to God, purify our conscience from dead works to serve the living God.

Hebrews 9:14

"Peace of conscience is nothing but the echo of pardoning mercy"

William Gurnall

CONSCIENCE
CLEARED

ONE OF THE most intriguing and sinister characters in Christ's crucifixion was Pontius Pilate. Pilate was the local Roman governing authority in Jerusalem. Being a man who despised the Jews, but forced to live among them because of his position, he would do anything he could to not get involved in a local matter. Especially, involving an itinerant, blue-collar preacher. Yet, Pilate's hand was forced by the Jewish officials and he became a part of the system that ultimately sent Jesus to the cross -- even though, he personally contended that Jesus was innocent of all charges levied against him. In fact, in the bold and grand act of defiance, he ceremonially 'washed his hands of Jesus'. Matthew 27:24 says, "So when Pilate saw that he was gaining nothing, but rather that a riot was beginning, he took water and washed his hands before the crowd, saying, "I am innocent of this man's blood; see to it yourselves."

What happens to Pilate after these events are open for debate. The Western Church has tended to make him a villain. The Eastern Church took more of a favorable view of Pilate, believing that later in his life he became a Christian. Another tradition, around his life, dealt with his obsessive hand washing after his interaction with Christ. No matter what he did, Pilate could not fully wash Christ's blood off his hands; he continued to have a guilty conscience. I have known some people like this down through the years.

What a relief to know that Christ's death on the cross, not only forgives your sins, but it clears your conscience. When Christ forgives our sins, He throws them as far as 'the east is from the west' (Psalm 103:12).

One way to know that forgiveness has been experienced fully is that your conscience is clear. If you are struggling with a guilty conscience, you might need to fully appropriate the forgiveness Christ has given to you. Further, if you know He has forgiven you of your sins, but you fail to forgive yourself, what good is that? People who fail to forgive themselves void the cross of its power and continue to 'wash their own hands'. Romans 8:1 says, "There is therefore now no condemnation for those who are in Christ Jesus." Live it.

Reflections

What are you still 'washing your hands over'?

Spend a moment thanking Christ for His forgiveness.

For while we were still weak, at the right time Christ died for the ungodly. For one will scarcely die for a righteous person—though perhaps for a good person one would dare even to die— but God shows his love for us in that while we were still sinners, Christ died for us.

Romans 5:6-8

God proved His love on the Cross. When Christ hung, and bled, and died. It was God saying to the world, "I Love you".

Billy Graham

VISON OF CHRIST
LOVE

*I*N SEPTEMBER OF 2006, Michael Stepien, was walking home from work in Swissvale, Pennsylvania, where he was the head chef of a restaurant. As he walked through an alley, he was robbed and murdered by a 16-year-old man. At the hospital, the family, devastated and overwhelmed, decided to donate his organs to others who might need them so that his life might live on in others. One of the recipients was a man named Arthur

Thomas, a father of four, who received Stepien's heart. Thomas was within days of dying before his heart transplant.

Ten years later, Stephien's daughter, Jeni, was about to get married. Like most girls, she dreamed of the day when her father would walk her down the aisle to her future husband. As the occasion approached, she decided to ask Arthur Thomas to walk her down the aisle. While she could not have her father, she could have his heart. Thomas agreed to Jeni's offer and not only walked down the aisle, but gave her a daddy-daughter dance at the reception and everything else she wanted. It was the least that Arthur could do, having been given life by Jeni's father.

Have you ever realized that someone has died for you? How humbling is that? Think about it. Jesus didn't die for generic mankind. He died for you. Just like the story above, one, named Jesus, died so that you could live. In fact, he died so that you could have a different heart. You could have a heart like His.

Yet, in the story, we are more like the 16-year-old criminal, Leslie Brown. The verse above said that 'while we were still sinners, Christ died for us.' We were not the man in the hospital awaiting the transplant, we were active sinners, like the murderer. It is amazing that Christ loves us at all, let alone while we were still sinning. We were lying, stealing, cheating, practicing immorality, and every other form of evil and still Christ loved us enough to die for us.

Just as Arthur was willing to stand-in as Jeni's Father when she called, how can we not do whatever Christ has called us to do considering all that He has done for us?

Reflections

What does it feel like to know Jesus willingly died for you?

What parts of you still need to be surrendered to Him?

For since the law has but a shadow of the good things to come instead of the true form of these realities, it can never, by the same sacrifices that are continually offered every year, make perfect those who draw near. Otherwise, would they not have ceased to be offered, since the worshipers, having once been cleansed, would no longer have any consciousness of sins? But in these sacrifices, there is a reminder of sins every year. For it is impossible for the blood of bulls and goats to take away sins.

Hebrews 10:1-4

"Christ's sacrifice was offered once, once for all, because by one offering, and that offered once, the sacrifice was carried out perfectly."

John Owen

NOTHING ELSE IS NEEDED

WHEN YOU LOOK in the Old Testament, you see the use of sacrificed animals to compensate for the sins of mankind. For instance, in the story of Adam and Eve, God, Himself, makes the very first blood sacrifice to cover the sins of the first couple. Genesis 3:21 says, "And the Lord God made for Adam and for his wife garments of skins and clothed them." We learn early in the story of redemption that blood is essential in making a payment for sin. God used an animal, the text does not say which kind, to make garments of clothing for Adam and Eve.

Then, as the Old Testament unfolds, the Tabernacle and later the Temple are set up as the place of sacrifice. Deuteronomy 12:5-6 says, "But you shall seek the place that the Lord your God will choose out of all your tribes to put his name and make his habitation there. There you shall go, and there you shall bring your burnt offerings and your sacrifices, your tithes and the contribution that you present, your vow offerings, your freewill offerings, and the firstborn of your herd and of your flock." It was in the Holy of Holies that the very presence of God dwelt in both places of worship.

Yet, in all the hundreds of thousands of sacrifices that happened in the hundreds of years that the sacrificial system was practiced, all those animals pointed to Jesus. It was his cousin, John the Baptist, who said it best when he introduced Jesus on the banks of the Jordan River by saying, "Behold, the Lamb of God, who takes away the sin of the world!" (John 1:29) Jesus was the perfect sacrifice once for all. Those worshippers in the sacrificial system all knew that one day the perfect sacrifice would come. So, their faith was not in an animal to remove sins, but a Messiah in the future. Therefore, there is no need for a sacrificial system because Jesus, the perfect Lamb of God, has provide, himself, as the perfect sacrifice for all who would believe in Him.

Reflections

Why is it important that we understand "Nothing else is needed"?

What is your sacrifice you bring to the alter instead of Jesus?

Made in the USA
Monee, IL
11 November 2021